With a warm heart for all people with (early-onset) dementia
and all those who love them for who they were, are, and remain.
Because there's love that never vanishes.

– An Swerts and Eline van Lindenhuizen

Written by An Swerts
Illustrated by Eline van Lindenhuizen

Dear Girl

Clavis

NEW YORK

"That will be fifty dollars for the doll, please,"
Grandpa says to the lady in front of the counter.
"Here you are," the lady answers while paying.

"Thank you," Grandpa says.
"Now you can go and enjoy your day.
I'll see you out."

"Yes, it truly is fine weather today," the lady says cheerfully,
while Grandpa courteously opens the door for her.
Then, he sees the doll in her arms.

"Excuse me, you have to pay for that," he says.
The lady is amazed. "But I *did* just pay," she replies angrily.
Grandpa looks confused, but Cathy nods.
"Oh, I'm very sorry," Grandpa says quickly.

"Oh! You've laid your reading glasses
between the dolls, Grandpa!" Cathy laughs.
"Have I really?" Grandpa asks.
"Boy, I'm pretty absent-minded these days."

That's true, Cathy thinks.
Grandpa loses things all the time.
And he forgets a lot—even things that just happened.

But Grandpa does remember things that happened when he was a child, very well.
Like that time he snuck into the priest's garden to go cherry picking,
and the maid chased him away. "Her cheeks were as red as . . . cherries!"
Grandpa always adds as his eyes twinkle with fun.

"Gustave, you have to see a neurologist," Grandpa's doctor says one day.
He looks at Cathy. "That's a doctor who knows a lot about the brain.
He'll give your grandpa a number of tests,
a bit like what you get at school.

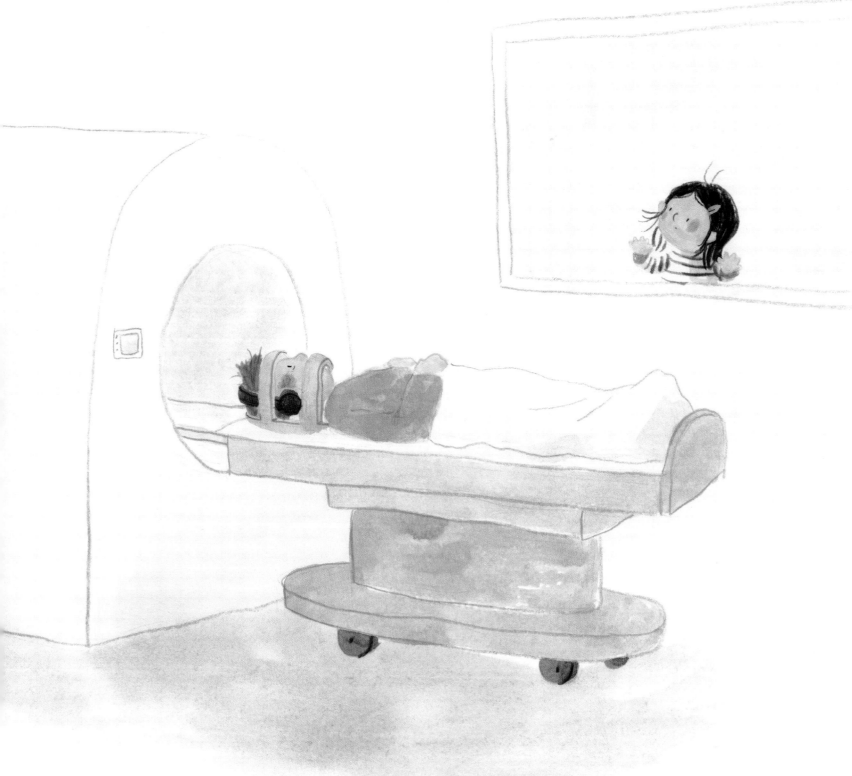

Your grandpa will also get a brain scan in a sort of tunnel.
He'll have on headphones to block out the noisy machine.
He'll be like an astronaut in a rocket.
That way, the doctor can take pictures of Grandpa's brain."
"Alright," Grandpa says. "I'll have my head checked."
He smiles at Cathy, but she notices that it isn't a cheerful smile.

They anxiously wait for the test results.
Finally, Grandpa's results arrive,
but it's not a good report.
Grandma's eyes look sad as she tells us
what the report says. "Grandpa has
an illness which makes it more and more
difficult for him to remember things."
"Like, what he's just done,
or where he puts things?" Cathy asks.
Grandma nods. "He may also forget
what words mean," she explains.

Cathy gives Grandpa a surprised look.
"When I tell you that I went to the beach,
you won't know what *beach* means?" she asks.
"That's possible," Grandpa sadly replies.

"Let's go to the beach right now," Cathy says firmly to Grandma.
"Good idea," Grandma says. "We deserve a trip after that news."
In chalk, Grandma quickly writes something on the blackboard
behind the shop's door. Then, she walks inside to get beach stuff.
Cathy reads what Grandma has written: *Closed early today for family reasons.*
Nobody will understand that, Cathy thinks.
She picks up the piece of chalk and writes underneath:
We have to go to the beach urgently.

On the beach, Cathy looks at Grandpa with determination.
Grandpa knows that this is how his Cathy looks when she has a plan.
"Grandpa, think very hard now," Cathy says. "What do *you* like most about the beach?"
Grandpa takes a moment and replies: "The sound of the waves and the seagulls and—"

"Okay," Cathy cuts him short. "Let's start with that."
And she walks to the water with Grandma's phone in her hand.
What on earth is she going to do? Grandpa asks himself.

The next day, Cathy wants to know
which scent Grandpa likes most.
If Grandpa forgets, she'll be able
to let him sniff his favorite scent.
She thinks that's important.
When she's sad, she holds
Soft Bear against her nose.
Soft Bear's scent always
helps her to feel better again.

"Well," Grandpa says. "I like the smell of . . . sweaty feet!"
His belly shakes with laughter. Cathy gives him a stern look.
"No, no," Grandpa quickly replies. "I love the smell of lavender."

A couple of weeks later, Grandma is busy with customers
when Cathy enters the toy shop. "Where is Grandpa?" she asks.
Grandma gestures in the direction of the storage room.
Grandpa sits on a stool with his head in his hands.
"What's wrong, Grandpa?" Cathy asks. She's concerned.
"What if I forget your name soon?" Grandpa asks quietly.
"Or worse, what if I don't remember that you're my granddaughter?"
His eyes fill with sadness.
"How would you call me then?" Cathy asks.
"What do you mean?" Grandpa replies.
"Well, when you've forgotten who I am," Cathy explains.
"How would you call me?"
Grandpa thinks for a moment.
"I would probably just call you *dear girl*," he says.
"That's fine with me," Cathy says cheerfully.
"And now we're going to do something nice!"
Grandpa's eyes smile again.

Just like previous years, Cathy goes on a trip abroad with Grandma and Grandpa during the summer holiday. And just like before, they have a lot of fun together.

They find the prettiest stones ever.

They build dams in brooks, just like beavers do.

They observe butterflies and dragonflies.

And they close each day with the same wonderful walk
through a large lavender field.

Things go well for a few more years,
until Grandpa starts to remember less and less.
Talking also becomes more and more difficult.
Of course, Grandma is there for Grandpa, but she also has to keep
their toy shop going. So, Grandma can't be with Grandpa all day long.
This is why Grandpa goes to an *assisted-living center*.
At first, he only lives there during the daytime, but soon he stays overnight.

In the assisted-living center,
there are *health care providers* day and night.
They look after Grandpa and the other residents,
and help them with the little everyday things.
They also have fun activities, so that everyone feels well.
Grandma pays Grandpa a visit every night.
Cathy accompanies her very often.
And today, Cathy definitely wants to come along,
since it's Grandpa's birthday!

When Grandma and Cathy arrive, Grandpa isn't in his room.
"He's in the garden!" Grandpa's neighbor shouts.
First, Grandma fills up his cookie jar and Cathy puts
a little bag of fresh lavender underneath Grandpa's pillow.
She knows that he'll sleep better that way.
They find Grandpa in the shadow of an ancient tree.
Cathy presses a big fat kiss on Grandpa's cheek.
"Happy birthday, Grandpa!" she says cheerfully.
Grandpa looks at her with surprise, but his eyes sparkle.
"Dear girl," he says. Cathy smiles from ear to ear.

"Today we went to the beach," Cathy tells him.
"Oh . . ." Grandpa just says.
Then, Cathy takes something out of her backpack:
the prettiest shell ever and a little bag of sand.
She pours some sand in Grandpa's hand. Grandpa smiles.
"Grandma, can I have your phone for a minute?" Cathy asks.
"Sure," Grandma says, and she winks.

A bit later, the blackbirds in the garden
are terrified when they hear seagulls scream.
"Beach . . ." Grandpa says.
"Right!" Cathy shouts with joy.
"Beach," Grandpa repeats. And then: "Wonderful."
"I agree, Grandpa!" Cathy says, and she puts her arms around him.
"The beach is wonderful. And we'll go there together soon."

Which path do Cathy and Grandpa have to follow to get to the beach?

At the beach you can hear, see, smell,
feel and taste all sorts of things.

Grandpa likes to hear the noisy seagulls.
Which sounds do you enjoy at the beach?

Do you see that sailing boat in the distance?
Cathy takes a photo of the boat.
How many seagulls do you count in the air?
How many buoys in the water?
And how many starfish and pebbles on the beach?

Do you like the smell of the beach?
And did you know that this very typical smell
is also caused by algae? Algae are green wisps
on the breakwater.

Do you enjoy it when the strong wind blows
in your face and hair on the beach?
Or do you prefer a light breeze?
**Today there's a fierce wind. Do you see that
girl who nearly lost her hat in the wind?**

Have you ever tasted splashing ocean water?
How would you describe the taste?
Are there other things at the beach you prefer tasting?
Maybe the snacks the beach vendor sells?
What would you like to buy from him?